Chatter in the Skull

H.T. Reynolds

BookLeaf Publishing

India | USA | UK

Chatter in the Skull © 2024 H.T. Reynolds

All rights reserved.

No part of this publication may be reproduced, stored in a retrieval system, or transmitted, in any form or by any means, electronic, mechanical, photocopying, recording or otherwise, without the prior written permission of the presenters.

H.T. Reynolds asserts the moral right to be identified as the author of this work.

Presentation by *BookLeaf Publishing*

Web: www.bookleafpub.com

E-mail: info@bookleafpub.com

ISBN: 9789363302273

First edition 2024

Inspired by the insights of Alan Watts, this poetry collection delves into the compulsive reckoning of thoughts from a neurodivergent mind struggling with what it means to be safe, free, a father, a man, and an American in a world that often feels detached from authenticity creating the need to find clarity amidst the noise.

NOT FRIENDLY

somewhere a chain snaps
                    taut
a father clocks in
purchases the bulk
of the training—
                    capitalism for dummies,
a tether,
            a dream
like the Saturday morning medley
he consumed young—dream big, princess

now, he consumes memories
of his family—
what's left,
                while at the office,
while in a car,
                while waiting motionless

the chafe of adapting:

                    chapter 7
learn to work
                    work hard
work between hobbies
                    work through dinner

chapter 8
family is an expense
you cannot afford

chapter 9
[purchase the next volume]

somewhere a father hangs up his chains,
clocks out,
                    dreams
while driving home to sleep,
listening to talk radio
                              for a talking point
he can use tomorrow

hoping to find his family
still awake
                    & waiting

SOMEWHERE IN AMERICA

a wife rocks her hips
reminding her man to return home

a capitalist deposits his harvested sweat
while a consumer buys it

a mother fits her sons for the new school year
outfits to match their caskets and burial plots

a priest cashes in his confessions,
joins his pilot, who knows the fastest routes

a tourniquet's fastened to the American dream
someone just suffered from

LOOKING BACK

I recall my first skinned knee,
how you drew me in, mother,
and we watched the red patch
blossom across my sweatpants
—tinge dark like my eyes

I watched you splinter
when I took your tears
ran for the woods
and became wild

I concealed the parts of my heart
that craved for your eyes to see me
unbroken—without these hands
that broke you—that broke everything

but you became ashes in my eyes,
my rage igniting your kindling heart—
a cautionary request your parents gave
you to exorcise me lest the devil inside
infects your chaste skin

THE SHOCK OF
ARTERIAL OPENING

does the cow ever consider
its own corpse,
and how you'll make it

was there ever an understanding
after it watched the head
of the line drop,

your favorite—
it thought—but did it ever question
the care you were offering

and how it would stop—
a skull shot retirement party
with mandated attendance

did the cow ever consider
its own corpse,
and how you'd consume it

BROKEN JAWS AND
FIRST AMENDMENTS

I think of how a jawbone detaches—
a boa swallowing a child,
or the way a child's jaw snaps
and adults grow silent—
mothers and fathers begin writing
stories Junior learns to tell

I think of the way marriage was political
before it grew romantic,
before flowers replaced dowries
and wooing meant arriving
with a credit card
and an Uber ride from the mall

I wonder about the sleeping arrangements
of the congressmen's kids,
if they feel safe on whichever floor
in whichever home they're in,
if they ever feel embarrassed
to be descended from their fathers

I wonder how their jaws will detach
when it's their turn to swallow children

WHILE ON FOOT

when I returned to this body,
the traffic lights cascaded,
erupted streams of color,

a doctor's waiting room,
an exposed arm

my mouth resumed,
dripped words like Spring sap,
a collection plate you cashed in,
every syllable and dream

a mind's buzzing clock,
a goodbye rendezvous

you parked,
I exited that state of mind,
picked up my wrist's matching umbrella
opened them both to the sun, began on foot
to where you'd never dare

WHEN IT STILL EXISTED

can we really reconcile holding
our children alongside our guns

that ringing war drum;
the one that pulses then hums
keeping us all fast asleep

such prey to feast upon—
charred remains of posterity

our skies ashen black,
time invalid like our backs
as we've lost the spine
to take back the meaning
of holding small hands safe
leading them into tomorrow

when it still existed

SIXTH THE CHARM

death rests among a sea of bare branches,
a garden of hours spent snapping her fingers,
closing graves that demanded to be full

the rain brings new dancing souls,
lightning captures spring
hearts like radishes bathed in the dark

pools of aging laughter,
bloom bouquets of bruising—
the way wisdom comes naturally

grated from burrowed bones
while the world becomes learned
yet, death remains unimpressed

hangs her robe from the sepulcher
adorned with hung sons sprawled into t's,
wrapping her hand around the aged scythe,

she breathes—ready—for this mass necrosis,
praying this extinction sticks
—a world devoid of humanity

POSTMORTEM POETRY

please,
I invite you to examine me:
this is my body

I permit you to cut me open—this time

*

begin with my eyes
how they could always see the difference
between touch,
recognize the value of white in the knuckle
and what kind of touch it meant
          or reflected darkness like a demon I
inherited
strapped down and kept stationary, oozed ink
over bruised skin
          collecting in the corners of my mouth,
waiting to be spit out

**

trace my nerves from my eyes to my muscles
how efficiently—instinctively—they conducted
my fear
becoming fiber optics that flinched my muscles
firm like armor

or copied the rabbits, or cats, how they'd always
leap ahead of the strike
          copied the mongoose who dared to eat
the cobra
hopping back legs with ruby eyes
chattering teeth that proved his loyalty to the
boy

***

examine my bones
                    and how they betrayed me
grew in on themselves—grew soft and brittle,
like home gets
when romance is involved
          or alcohol—or both
I became a wooden doll, hanging from calloused
hands—
          working hands—man's hands that knew
just how to play rough

****

run your hands over my skin
                    how it was never a match for
concrete
a constellation of vows exchanged with each
consummation
I do—she'd say
and I would come undone

bleed until she permitted me to stop, would
return me home to mother
          who would remove her skirt and finish
what the concrete started

*****
expose my abdominal cavity
                how I was just another
participant in addiction
          my liver a deposit of faith in the wrong
person
a stomach that could never handle sympathy, or
masculinity,
or the intricacies of opening carcasses
skinning them clean, carving them up for dinner
plates
          withdraw these bones—my
inadequacies—I was forced to swallow

******
move up and open my thoracic cavity
you'll find where my heart became a chrysalis
her love the torch
where I burned upon birth, allowed my new
wings to singe
to turn stillborn baby blue, into another of her
memories
a once-upon-a-time-I-used-to kind of story—as a
cautionary tale

reserved for her own kids

****

return to my face
                pull open my mouth
see how my tongue became a carpet
and your souls became clean
read about my death in the paper the next day
how I bled out
        but kept your secrets despite the
medication

please,
see all of this—

                                            my

body

I permit you
open me

BAPTISM

14

her mouth exhales winter—
the contents of her stomach,
baptizing me with an end to summer

her hands clutch at her mouth—
a black rose erupts from her throat,
plants itself between her thighs

I remove it,
        remind her it was never ours,
and take us home

SOLITARY BLEEDING

She swallows night like lithium—
consuming him—becoming a used
exposure with each flashbulb—
a broken home dissolving into her.

She soothes her barreling pulse,
her timid breasts into leftover
breaths fading away. The dragon
erupts into each gasping vein, this
bare night hiding her heart's rhythm—

a vacancy Hotel chain—alone,
with her bleeding brain.

PAUL

what is your favorite breath?
the first;
before you knew its meaning
the last;
when you learn its worth

could it be the ones given freely;
points that chase youth away,
spurts that swat flies that try
to sneak between your teeth

could it be the air between skin
echoing in the dark—lovers
searching for the right words,
breathlessly giving them life

could it be the one you held—that night,
when doors shred apart,
sobbing against cat fur
to keep your breathing discrete

but his eyes found you,
serrated your skin
before you faded—watching from above
his frantic breathing

could it be that your favorite is not your own,
but the one that whispers
father—
as you never could

INDOCTRINATION

how many of you learned young
moms and dads aren't fun,
weren't designed to be played with

or perhaps you learned they are
serpents seeking prey
and you looked awfully tasty

fangs that remained embedded in
the meat of your exposed thigh—
embraces that never quite broke clean

how you found your own teeth fitting
together in new ways—broken
ribs and what was contained between

how many of you learned young
moms and dads aren't fun
weren't designed to be

PLOT POINTS
pt. II

you broken hip-popotamus

you engorged welfare prince

stand, right before the leg loss
the limp shrimp, skimping on walking,
planting the wheel and carriage,
collecting Uncle Sam's deposit

we propose a prosthetic-procedure
fixed and tight-laced

boy
lift your leg,   let us separate
the sinew from view—
string muscle to thread, weave
and conceal with hanging sheets,
stickers for covering clots
drooping from mirrors

we forgot—
registers pay it out; mother—
the one capable of writing your name
for you   —the healing,

all yours—a cast system,

you know,   your legs, they
spread open—easy,
barred, spaced out—no entry
for sidewalks, no time for a race,
the traction on your heels
can deliver the
pace

yourself lad,
your thighs eroded off the plate
and separated, they found the water
dish, soak tub—sea-salted, buoyant,
a miracle week-end

why so keen to age, lad
there's one thing we can shoot you with—
a syringe that grows your balls back,
since your legs work, we must measure
your distance above dirt—

above or below,
just know the trigger exists
with her lips she whispers with—
cute portraits, coming attractions,
blushing eyes—tempt the weaker
lad, like flotsam who heeded her cries
this is what your balls will realize

once they've sprouted a matching cock

let her burn your body, boy
for we are anchored young and
your face will be a grimace soon enough—
just take her hands, trace your epitaph
at chest-level, dripping ropes of blood
alive like the razor,   the gun

your halo for a chair—a throne,
swap it out—press firm, draw the lines deep
eject the casings—breathe out the smoke

linger,
wait
cope—harder

just stitch yourself up
grow your legs back
become a man
read it from a book
learn to smile

look, lad,
you took your time—
now breathe,   survive

WHAT CAN'T BE LOST

when I was young
I wondered what power was
and when I'd get some

I believed it was the measure
of a man and how much
he could see over—
his reach on high shelves

then I believed it was the weight
he could carry, how far he could take
it, the way he owned it, threw it around

I thought it was her (whoever)
how she'd swoon over my masculinity

but then

the years drew lines on my skin
and I found poetry

ALONG CAME A SPIDER

just because we don't travel in the dark
corners beneath baseboards and
cabinets doesn't mean there isn't traffic,
a chorus of commotion—a horde

just ask the spider who sets up its net,
hides the seams between dreaming
and the twinkling overhead light
that keeps the kitchen from darkness

it's had success capturing creatures
content with existing in shadows
for without the morning cobwebs,
we'd never know night existed

UNDRESSED WORDS & TONGUES

I like to read your words real slow-like
unbutton every b-eat, inspect the t-ease
to ensure they're crossed and animated

what'd you say, dear?
the bottom's comin' loose?

well, try and stand-a-second,
unfold each vowel,
let them hang—wrinkle
in the wind just right

that'll calm your nerves

let them see into those o-st,
those cantaloupes growin' firm
understanding the rind and seeds,
your job to plant 'em
to scatter 'em line by seam
to stream rows of verses crossed
lengthwise

then, I'll swallow what you said, dear
I'll count each scar
trace 'em along your skin—brand 'em,

expose the sutures that were there

even now, you form them beautifully
spellin' 'em out—
words that reach
deep inside me
—just right

DEAR DECAPITATED
RABBIT

return home, swallow
me whole, feel the lick
of my wicked kiss

forming your words,
plucking out your organs
finding joy in dissecting—

identifying every orifice
satiating my curiosity
understanding why rabbits

disembody themselves,
injecting every drop of sun
to lose their heads

but I hear it's beautiful
when your bodies coat the blades
of grass a saturated red,
glistening fire I could drink
through your throat

APRIL

to the family who chose
to reside beside the creek
for the ambiance,
the wildlife,
the solitude of summer

are there moments of regret
when the Pennsylvania spring
rises into a river
and destroys almost everything

WHEN I BECOME A PILGRIM

an ethereal journeyman,
keep those whispers
clenched between portraits

slip them beneath the times
I held cold hands to warm hopes
staring at starlight

when I captured your attention
with matching eyes—the catalyst
for my heart to survive—a birthed oath

keep those pasted photographs on walls,
letters haphazardly strewn across the floor
sticking to the points we wore through

hours of longing amidst stones and stories
among thoughtless roses and fading breaths
regrets through tears and carelessness

the last time a hand graced this sepulcrum
silence preceded the burden of living
ceilings up, tables full, stomachs comfortable

and yet the gasp that I left was the apology
my promise of setting up the blocks
only to knock them over

so, when I find solace in effervescence,
a candescence of thought erupting
into pageantry through constellations

when I shed those silences, our embraces,
keep those tokens close
to where my words once would be

DISTENDING

where does all that growing come from
the way your bones lengthen
into just the right amount of skin,
fibers that hold your mind in place
as it washes itself with the world,
drinking it in just a little at a time…

then my ambition devours all reason
and there is a man at my door walking in
and the sun's rusty halo washes his back
and I see how worn his hands have become

LAST BLOOD

the last time I was bleeding
it was raining

against the chilled bus window
hiding me from the outside

my thin skin becoming
kid's cavalier laughter
despite me

I held back what I could

allowed the rest to flow
over hoping the rain would find
its way in—saturate me sterile

nobody cared

I deserved it

the bleeding
the rain
will stop

that's what they say   right

FICKLE MIND: CHILD, RUN

I watched my mouth—in my mind—transform,
distort into vibration and teeth
a thin ring of distended cracks and erosion red

a beast spoke—from my lungs—in my mind,
poured out the sickly bromine to calm
but it kept the flames from permeating

I watched her smile shatter, her eyes falter,
glimpsing—into my mind—my capacity
for carnage

LAUGHTER LIKE RAIN

why does your pattering laughter
carve pockmarks into my spine
like the rain's crescendo—
an eruption of its collective weight
how we'd watch the earth struggle
to keep up,
sobbing streams
that rushed into torrents we'd fail
to follow,
trying to make sense of sound
like it was uninvited conversation
we just couldn't create space for,
but you say it's water
it's life,
it's clean,
it's harmless

but I shared every drowning I endured—

when silence was safer—a raft,

I'd always fear would fill
to sinking

WHEN DEATH COMES

she will smile like my mother

stroke my soiled hair
hum and paint my eyelids closed
fasten them to sleep—
tether me to the stars

when death comes
she will hold me like my mother

rock me on warn oak chairs
with cigarette burns and creases
on my exposed skin—a collapsing
sun—a shedding moon

when my mother comes
she will greet me like death

like a garden of blossoming stones
like a singed birth certificate
like how, when I was a child
I sought them both

POCKETWATCHING

his wool pocket
filled with chewed gum;
lines that linger on his lips
like film on a stale pond

opening with each under-bed shoebox—
the one with an unloaded gun and stained noose,
a nude photo of a woman through an open door,
antique pennies without their uses,
a collection of Polaroids—sunshine beach poses,
the trout held by its gaping mouth

he was the type to remind you of your shoes
—where they've been,
the loose aspirin at the bottom of mother's purse

just take it, dear

he was that guy,
who'd describe the shifting sun in verse,
chew it,
place it in his wool pocket
with his loaded gun

STARBURSTS

do you ever wish for a starburst
when I can only give you the rain
a cardboard boat to cross the pool
instead of a bench to avoid the pain

are you ever saddened
by the way we are so careful—
how we secured every outlet,
pocketed the power you'll grow into
eventually, seeing the windows and
the doors as the bolted barracks—
the bulletproof American dream,
without the ganja to survive
the colorless arrangement we've devised

will you ever accept our receipts
for each protection purchased

will you ever be who you choose
despite me

IN THIS, I BELIEVE

37

I remove the dark   red clotted skin
drop it into mounds—
this tithe taken
for another try

Today   I breathe
Tomorrow   I'll die

This razor ally—
my mind a weed garden
collected to burn,
because God loves me

Today   I eat
Tomorrow   I'll die

My dear—my lovely—my
frightened lady at my altar,
amend my portrait,
transplant me—somehow

Today   I dream

        Tomorrow   I'll die

We stand bare upon each other's esteem
these exposed seconds
pass, and what's left
but to redress the decision,

Today   I believe

              Tomorrow   I'll die

I paint you my claret explanation
to suffice an apology
my deceiving tongue whispering
one day I'll be happy, too

In this moment—
I must believe that's true

Tomorrow   I'll die
Today   I'll be

AWAKING VIOLET

I'm told my vision looks angry
that I'm not seeing straight

I ask if they've ever seen violet
how she transforms in light—

red in the dark and blue with shadow
how she rolls over,

opens into wounds—
cavities she shows truth through

they tell me I'm overthinking
that I haven't met her family yet

but they've already bathed in gray
shed whatever color was left

I've already collected the bathwater
pulled violet from its depths

doused my room with her breath
and drew my curtains,

until dawn broke
and I could see again

MAY I BE FOUND

if I lose to myself,

take aim
oh, brilliant wings,
fold and shatter
beneath gravity—
disintegrate

oh, ire be tame,
dissolve into crystal springs,
calcify and scatter,
accumulate into cavities—
composed

oh, may I be found
scar-less,
a chrysalis shell
      casing echoing—
tempered cold

CHALK AND CONVERSE

things don't always fall when dropped
like your attention,   for example,
or affection
they just   carry on to the next thing

but that's cool
we continue to pick up the rocks
they leave us with
put them in our heads
continue through
the mazes
they scold us for getting trapped in
as if we knew of a solution
but we're just living off breadcrumbs
the other sorry shit left
to navigate with

but that's cool
the air will always grow   denser
right before lightning stops our hearts
feet becoming grounded in glass,
finally finding something firm
to stand on

but that's cool

we never needed our lungs
without our veins
an empty tape deck refusing
to rewind itself
and just like that—
we snap our fingers,
take our turn at the turret,
put the gag back in our broken mouths,
sit back down and tremble

we pick up the chalk   outline ourselves

but that's cool   it's all we know to do

PASSING BY

I don't believe in forever,
for even the serenity of nothing
was disturbed by creation

but who are we
to displace such peace—
a mere wave awaiting

its turn to break,
fade, and return
again to nothing

MARIE

with your diamond eyes
and cavernous appetite,
I'm right next to you,   red,
bled out and strangled blue

a hollowed-out gunshot wound,

with wrists
unpackaged—
tape-strung up and ragged

teeth
serrated–speaking freshly ground apologies
satiated
         lump-en-dick-to-mes   collected
assembled from your bones I ectomied out
                  —surgically precise

your pulse recorded with that band's debut
         broadside single filed down
                  your skirt   served—
that cache of stones   I purged

threw out like bones,   shaken and cast–
futures told between that nail
and broken glass

POETRY IS

a throbbing, oozing wound

but who are the ones
at the keyboards bleeding,
and the ones watching
how red shifts
with the light—
the pulse & skin
contracting

the other hand
grasping,
holding the blood back

we—mere eyes—
watch as it pours
wondering where it'll land,
who will clean it up,
will it ever stop

but who finds death,
recalls each scar's origin
on their own body
those thoughts
tempering their skin

watching the hand
pressing harder,
beginning to hurt—
to feel like healing

poetry is that open wound
stitched closed
reminding us
it no longer matters

ANGEL

when she tells you to put cock sounds
in your poem, you grow them like carrots
feel your throat clench and the tongue bulge
create the cacophony of elongated growls
like cats clawing their way to finishing

when she tells you to bring in the go
the green signal's glow giving you permission
to glaze over that smooth galvanized concrete
a glorious collection of cluster fucks

when she rings that bell rough, that bark,
king, you better be listening to everything
that pulse beat of your carotid artery
that choke of your throat from swallowing

grow green, loudly, stiffen that orange coat,
carrot proud, overshadow the legumes
that claw and cling, coil around like nooses
but don't let them hang you, cub,
for she says you've got some growing to do

FIRST STEPS

be the kind of guy who knows what he wants—

coffee with four teaspoons of sweet cream
dreams that mean the world,

the way the sun lassos leaf buds
on its way to the sky
how the freshly paved asphalt
melts into your lungs
rubs the tires of your car like a lover
—smooth ride dive into music

but there is only so much a man can stomach
so much he can stand…
at the edge of this carousel
and you could just step off

but then,

 you learned how the world revolves around the
sun
—spinning,

and nobody's told you
how to step off

VILLAIN AM I NONE

I wore her trespasses on my body
thinned out—an elongated coping
mask worn like a bandage
concealing her splinters I evacuated
from my throat—
carved promises into my arms
a plea to father, God—

it's hard to hold my heart
villainous when you were never there

APOPTOSIS AND AFTERBIRTH

we become weeds when we hit the air—
perhaps even before that,
when we divide ourselves
into too many pieces
exchange our mother's dreams
for its calcium

we learn to walk, to refuse apoptosis—
throw on our shades
innovate our arrogance
plunge our fists
into the earth
and multiply—
a cancerous growth
dissolving our afterbirth

earth spits and coughs—
feels its skin tingling,
seeks a doctor,
but they, too,
may succumb
to humanity

BETWEEN THE LINES OF MY POETRY

will you despise me
for the words I've written down
instead of speaking to you

will you learn to read between
the lines of my poetry
to see my point of view

will you find those treasure maps—
adventures we never got around to
settling instead for paper substitutes

will you forgive this old ghost
whose poems were all that he left
as an inheritance to you both

WITHOUT ME

someday
you'll see a world without me
and I hope it's everything
you wanted

perhaps
I'll walk through your mind
while the sun's still dreaming
of lovers and filling diaries

but I will be somewhere
the light is not

A LIFE WELL-FED

at night,
I placed my daughter into her crib
drew the small blankets to her chin
set my heavy eyes toward the morning
retired to my chamber, pulled the silence
to my chin, welcomed the streetlights in
to sing me to sleep, meeting me in my dreams

when I woke,
my daughter stirred cubed apples into my
oatmeal
prepared herself an omelet with chives
read the paper to me over our breakfast
reiterated the spots I forgot and rearranged
discussions of mortality until I had finished
eating
allowed the nurses in with syringes and
stethoscopes
spoke to them with gazes and gestures

at night,
my daughter placed me back in bed
drew the sterile blanket to my chin
set her heavy eyes toward mourning
& watched me reunite with her mother

DREAMS OF FLYING

let me take your z's
construct you a zoo,
take your bars
& build you an aviary

so you can keep your wings clean

sleep,
& I can find
an empty cage
in the morning

FOLLOWING SNOW

it falls,
covers,
coats
my thoughts
a sidewalk that was once
there
peppered with prints—
exposed concrete
where I was,
once
a sketch outline against bare snow
gathering my mind
blank
its weight holding me
like gravity,

my mass evaporates
into printed skylines
dusted lights dancing
between flakes,
taking away that ache
concealed beneath
glowing surfaces—
ice-diffused candles
a dancer spared the density of storms

EULOGY

she sat, knees to chin, eyes fixed on last night,
those hands that cradled her, bathed her
with purple bruises, fitted her with skirts
to cover her spoiled legs, each turn, every spin
the way she allowed herself to blossom open,
the shoes staying on, the music staying on,
her eyes closing as she erupted into hollow

her gaze became the center of the room
her lips the permeating incense
that dripped over muted conversations
from chalkboards to polished
desks that swallowed her completely

I wish I'd noticed

I wish I'd found her before she fell

I wish I'd have seen her father's shackled grin
    before it bound her to suffering

I wish I'd spoken before words were exchanged
    over her box, her portrait—silent pews

she was the way the sun felt when spring

demanded its turn

her eyes still the center of the room
even while closed

SITTING UPON A PARK BENCH IN OCTOBER

don't erase an old man's words—
his bones and weary marrow

sit a bit longer, son
watch the tree line for a moment,
just dwell without that silicone

see how the land curves
indents into forests
how it waits to be touched,
explored from the inside

tell me your stories, son
those breathless nights dancing
upon lawns strewn with diamond webs
waiting to catch your words

while I dig my bed—a tomb
filled with pick-up sticks
we held like guns
fired until the day turned red

linger a moment longer, son
let the day set to night,

occupy this space I reserved
—nearly empty

don't erase an old man's words—
let them sit a bit longer
let them fall and settle

DUBIOUS

someone always sees you
not pick up your dog's shit

somehow finding a way
to see every out-of-turn wave
made to a stranger

every time you check your teeth
in the rear-view mirror

the moment you sneeze
and just a chunk of phlegm
launches awkwardly out

somehow, they see all of this
but never those moments
when your skin aches
for embrace—
your soul's fire in need
of stoking, kindling pieces
of affirmation

somehow, they miss those moments
where you hold open the elevator door
for the man with full hands

the time you make a funny face
to soothe a screaming child
held over its mother's shoulder
as she balances her world on the other

they never find the time to piece together
every sigh you mask with,
every smile stapled on
like you learned from the tutorial

every conversation starter from the manual
on small talk in your back pocket

they will never know the contents
of your character—the fire in your heart

for they'll never ask,
and you'll never tell them

YOU ATE ME
DELIBERATELY

did you want to see me broken—
a soldier's coat, an unhonored one,
undertaker,   secret keeper,
mute calligrapher waiting for lean winter
to end

what caused us each to live hidden,
driven to opposite coasts   through
flowers and limestone daisies,
chalk-drawn centerlines
laying down   a perfect memory

why do I forget you loved me,
mistranslated from your journal entries
maybe I misread   you   completely
where one plus one equals everything but
—such savory secrets

but what can be used again   sinks
down to where it can be harvested
but I loved you in slow, dimwitted ways,
with you hardly speaking

a grindstone glut of privilege—

you ate me
daily   —deliberately

WELCOME TO THE MACHINE

when I look at my son
I find myself along his margins

my own eyes shine from my daughter's
seeing my body crumble—bleed

but this machine demands blood
—you'll see
and dear children,
none of this is fair

WICKED ARE THE WOLVES

your calcified wolf flesh—
a rusted-nail enclosure,
eyes scarred closed—stripped
words like crushed shell armor
adorning your busted collar

broken whisperer—kind
gentleman—word weaver;
birth her your blanket promises,

raise them like you mean it

clenching your teeth
that hold her safe

—still

STORYTIME

sixteen years sober—
tell me that story,
direct your world into view

what do you see
within that hindsight
with those bare bottles,
the shots empty and dry—
the damage done

how many circles does your calendar have
does your family speak of them,
think of them enough
to trust you again
can you feel their glances from the corners
as you pretend not to

do you ever wake in the morning
with that taste still there
somewhere
between your nasal cavity
and your tongue

DARKNESS DANCES

we once inhaled a cool night moon

cut from a tired velvet night
where I kept my fatherly advice

expired smiles—tenebrous strays
strung high as starlight

we sang softly—filled the dark,
humming goodnight

POETS ARE CHILDREN

look at what i made
mommy,   mommy,
mommy,

but then,   why,
why should we age
when the sun already leathers our skin
why should time take our drawings—
that alphabet we gave to the womb
we celebrate with feet firm on her skin
and arms extending—screaming:
see me stars,   galaxies,
mother,   i'm here,

in your eyesight within range—
of reach,   hold me
wrap me in that shine

notice how i persist   stand,
defy gravity
let it pull me
day   after   fucking day
just so that my blood pumps, again
tomorrow

notice when i fall—my knees blur
& bleed

to feel anything but the gravel
i remove each night before i sleep
just to keep the sheets clean
because you told me

you said that blood
ruins the color,
but blood is all i have to give

it hungers to be seen—devoured

mommy,

poets are children

waiting with their arms raised
dripping dots of ink
into lines and letters—
wrists that won't get better

eyes believing in sunlight
feeling gravity
waiting—to get picked up

TO SMILE WITHOUT
HURTING

I wanted to run my arms through
the shirt sleeves you left me with

to wrap them around those chairs
we used to place back-to-back—
pretend you were the damsel,
and I the prince

I recall how you used to open yourself,
desire to smile without hurting

I'd hold open your edges,
listen to its dripping malcontent,
spend hours assuaging your parents' negligence
and endure the desolation it left me with

I'd stitch closed the moment—
a collection of perjured teeth

we'd return to our chairs,
serve each other our tithing
—my pound of flesh
for your wedding dress

I accumulated those years
onto lines on paper,

held onto your vacancy
between the bend of metal
and where it served as a tourniquet—
a blistering infected pocket

but I understand now,
that desire to smile without hurting

but my arms no longer catch
on those sleeves you left me with—
a blouse with no color left,
a photograph of another life

               purged,
and discarded

AWAY THESE CHILDISH THINGS

when you're a child
you do not understand a broken body
until you do
shoulders, knees, and toes
a blistered spine
a chair
a cage
a place to stay

a bed
a casket
a place to rest
until one day
the morning wanes

to a broken body

CANCER COLLECTOR

for the first time
        I put God down
and made a wish

for your daughter
        to get a puppy—
a gift card

so she can handle the leukemia

the days Bagster
can't lick sense
into her suffering

perhaps I'll pick God back up,
interrogate him properly,
throw the book at him

demand to know

how many bodies
will pay his toll

RIGHT TO WORK

they teach us to whistle while we work,
to fill our way through cemeteries—
we canary in the mines

but there's something wrong;
we keep dying

so they order more canaries,
show us the carcasses,
and put us back to work

THE CHICKADEE KNOWS

what do the trees think
when they look at our homes—
old oak bones

do they grieve

I suppose the chickadee knows,
dwelling within old oak bones

DAY ZERO

have you ever watched a star form
witness her edges glisten
her corners mold into shine
the rhythm of her heart
adapting to your gaze
all the ways she'll learn to radiate
trace patterns against the night
compete with the sun and its light
the years it'll take to hear her speak
of grand days and majestic
moments of her youth
alive and glimmering
with a pulse so bold to be told
there are only so many colors
she's allowed to see

GOD IS IN THE RAIN

I watch God in your eyes,
little captured drops sliding
across your point of view
creasing your silent lips

your rushing waves,
a reluctant sky,
corroded loose skin
dropping like aprons—
like the conversation
that led us here

you draw your fingers
across my throat,
drink in the night
wait for me to come along,
share in your little death
find our resuming pulse

the fearful morning waits
to stain the soil clean
with sunlight
with rain

LOBBY REUNIONS

he kept her within the creases of his eyes
his smile lines and the folded ridges of his hands
that pulled the chair out from the table—

picking up with the conversation

the lobby
stone carried him to my corner
his eagerness that settled like dust
eroding the sands he has left,
content
in the way he speaks in sips and smiles
staring off into that hazy longing
finding her hands still across the table
once more
that laughter that always managed to catch
him smiling along,
that halo of a setting sun
wrapping her up
delivering her to him with each
whispered goodnight
until sleep took her away
placed her into his eyes,
carved lines with each day
that passed between them

in muted conversations—
sips and smiles

within this bustling lobby,
he spends his days waiting
for her who said goodnight
so long ago

VERSES

I find poetry
between small fingers
clutching the world,
opening windows,
keeping the air
from closing the doors,
focusing on the walls
and the bare ceiling

that holds all the stars

WINTER'S COAT

the way you coat your lungs
like it's winter and you're already cold
grounded below stale January air
clawing through life
as yours slips to vapor

just breathe it in again,
that saturated carcinogen

A SENSE TO PART WITH

can you still smell that Bud Light mint
I used to quiet myself,
to become entirely someone else

can you still taste me on your skin,
your lips from each murmur
slipped through a miasmatic amour

can you still hear my voice promise,
agree to ignore the volatile weather
the first time we slept with our backs together

ANOTHER LINE BORN

84

when another life ends,
a poet scratches a new line

and even happy poems
end with shovels